C000180369

SPIRIT OF THE

HIGHLAND PONY

HEIDI M. SANDS

First published in Great Britain in 2010

Copyright text and photographs © 2010 Heidi M. Sands

British Library Cataloguing-in-Publication Data
A CIP record for this title is available from the British Library

ISBN 978 1 906887 76 6

PiXZ Books
Halsgrove House, Ryelands Industrial Estate,
Bagley Road, Wellington, Somerset TA21 9PZ
Tel: 01823 653777
Fax: 01823 216796
email: sales@halsgrove.com

An imprint of Halstar Ltd, part of the Halsgrove
group of companies
Information on all Halsgrove titles is available at:
www.halsgrove.com

Printed and bound in China by Toppan Leefung Printing Ltd

Introduction

In 2005, after a lifetime of involvement with other breeds of native pony, Mansefield Mariandle came into my life. She was, and still is at the time of writing, the ride of a lifetime for my daughter.

Mandy as she is affectionately known at home was born in 1987, a grey dun Highland pony, with a pedigree of perfection including the great Swannidene. She introduced me and my family to the breed, one of steadfast loyalty with a kind generous nature, rugged wild beauty and utmost ability.

The Highland pony breed stands between 13hh and 14.2hh. Some ponies show a dorsal stripe along their backs or zebra markings on their legs giving away their primitive origins. The range of dun colours within the breed is amazing. Foals born with mouse, grey, yellow or cream dun coats can very often lighten as they grow older, turning grey. With other coats of solid colours including brown, black, grey and the occasional chestnut, there is something for everyone.

With staggering ability as ridden, driven and working ponies bringing deer off the hill, the 'garron' as the Highland is sometimes known can turn its hoof to most things. The greatest show of these ponies is undoubtedly at the Royal Highland Show at Ingliston near Edinburgh in June each year. Other highlights include the breed show, but it is on the studs, out on the hills, in show rings, fields and paddocks that this special breed stands proud.

Designated by the RBST as 'at risk' category 4, it is to the increasing number of enthusiasts of the Highland pony that we look to for the future of this breed as it trots out, into and through the twenty first century.

A curious youngster at Auchernack near Grantown on Spey takes an interest in the camera.

Opposite page:
A fine example of a good pony head with a kind eye.

A Highland pony grazes near Newtonmore at the foot of the
Cairngorm range of mountains.

A real Highland beauty.

And a stretch before standing up again.

Opposite page:
A well balanced pony is paramount and has evolved over many generations of breeding.

At 17 years old Arran shows a head full of wisdom.

Opposite page:
Champion Highland at the Royal Northern Spring Show the 3-year-old Morven of Coynach.

Champion Highland Monty O' the Glens at Elgin mart.

Child riders on the Ormiston ponies at Newtonmore with the snow-speckled Cairngorms as a backdrop.

Coming to call at
Glenlivet.

Connachan Buzzard, a 1995 born gelding sired by Highfield Glen Albyn, bred by
Mrs ME MacPherson waiting to go into his class at Perth.

Coordy of Birnam waiting to be judged.

Cuileann of Drunrui showing a lovely length of stride desired for ground clearance within the breed.

Dappled sunshine under the trees at the Mill House, Cluny Castle shows off the glossy summer coat of this pony, which shines with health.

Deer saddles, used to bring carcasses down off the hill on the backs of Highland ponies both in the past and today.

Do our bums look big in this?

Opposite page:
Elidh shows off her flexibility as well as her rare mouse dun colouring.

Enjoying a good roll to help get rid of a winter coat.

Erray Ash a 14-year-old stallion born and bred on the Island of Mull shelters in his trailer at the Spring Show at Thainstone.

Fiona Laing's Charlie trots out in spite of a rainstorm.

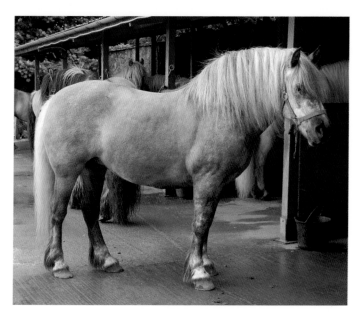

Fiona of Glenshiel, a 16-year-old cream dun mare, owned and used by Ben Alder estate as a deer stalking pony throughout the stalking season.

Greys come in many shades.

Haltered and dozing next to mum,
a Whitefield youngster.

Highland pony trekking with
novice riders showing the
breed's willingness and
surefooted ability over their
native terrain.

Highland in the highlands at winter turnout.

If you have an itch you simply have to ease it on the nearest tree no matter who's on board.

In the wonderful setting of the Ormiston family's Newtonmore Riding Centre, Highland pony x 'Tzar' in early training for vaulting, shows his skills at a fun day.

Judge Richard Deptford gives a thorough evaluation to a competitor.

Just wanting to say
'hello'. Highlands are
a friendly lot.

Opposite page:
Let's go – having fun at
the Ormiston family's
Newtonmore Centre.

Macdonald of Birnam, a 15-year-old yellow dun on his way home after exercise.

Mansfield Mariandle in the snow.

Much-loved family pony
Charlie waits patiently at
Archiestown in Moray.

Opposite page:
Molly of Dounemount,
a real show girl.

Newtonmore Riding Centre, home of the Ormiston family.
It was from this area in 1952 that the origins of pony trekking
began with the present custodian's grandfather
Ewan Ormiston.

Opposite page:
On the move at Lynchat in the highlands, these two ponies
instigated a rodeo amongst their cattle companions before
heading off uphill.

Panniers, once an essential piece of pony equipment out on the hill or on the farm and still in use on some estates.

Out in the heather at Rothiemurcus an American guest has his first experience of riding a Highland pony.

Pricked ears when trotting is always a good sign.

Social interaction is important between ponies – here one rubs its head on the other as they move forward.

Seen from above the full extent of the Highland dorsal stripe.

Resting in the sunshine with a friend.

Tacking up, Feona Laing prepares a pony at the Rothiemurcus trekking centre.

Opposite page:
Still striding out at Aberlour after a ride along the Speyside Way.

Yearling colt Glenglasshauagh of Alltnacriche finds something
of interest over the hedge.

Opposite page:
Three friends. Cairns Garlinebeg with Scaraben of Auchincrieve behind
and the handreared Cairns Guireaman to the right.

Waiting in the sunshine for their turn in the ring at Elgin mart.

Some ponies show zebra markings on their legs.

Waiting patiently in the stall at Newtonmore. Stalls are less common than they used to be – many ponies are now stabled in loose boxes.

HM the Queen, Patron of the Highland Pony Society and breeder of the Balmoral ponies, at the 2009 Royal Highland Show.

Opposite page:
An unusual sight in the Highland pony ridden classes at the 2009 RHS was Magnus of Brathens ridden sidesaddle.

Winner of the 2009 Sanderson trophy, a competition held between the
Champions of Scotland's four native breeds of horse and pony each
year at the RHS, Tower Gypsy Meg.

Opposite page:
Miss Anne Mitchell's unusually marked grey dun stallion
Dunedin Marksman at the RHS.

HM The Queen with the Sanderson Trophy at the 2009 RHS.

Opposite page:
A traditional turnout at the RHS.

A correctly fitted deer saddle.

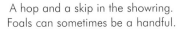

A hop and a skip in the showring.
Foals can sometimes be a handful.

Fit for a day on the hill.

The stallion Moss-Side Lairig Ghru.

Opposite page:
Ponies are still used on many Scottish estates to carry deer carcasses off the hill.
Some shows encourage correct turnout of such ponies with suitable classes.

A mare and foal wait patiently at a show – qualities are often learned by
foals from their dams which stand them in good stead for their futures.

Thea of Sherriffmoor with her stylish handler. Turnout is important for both pony and handler in the showring.

Reserve Champion at Turriff show in Scotland's NE in 2009 was Gordon and Anne Town's filly Pamela May of Forglen.

Opposite page:
Line up of dun ponies.

Lean on me. It's hard work waiting for mum.

Stripped and ready for the judge.